MANAGIN

MANAGING CHANGE

by Jeremy Thorn

The Industrial Society

First published 1986 by
The Industrial Society
Peter Runge House
3 Carlton House Terrace
London SW1Y 5DG
Telephone: 01–839 4300

Second edition 1989
Reprinted March 1990
© *The Industrial Society, 1986, 1989*

ISBN 0 85290 440 1

British Library Cataloguing in Publication Data
Thorn, Jeremy
Managing Change.
1. Organisational Change . Management aspects
I. Title II. Series
658.4'06

Typeset by Columns Ltd, Reading
Printed and bound in Great Britain by Belmont Press, Northampton

CONTENTS

FOREWORD

Whatever the discipline or level of management, the responsibilities of managers are many and various. It is their job to produce results with essentially just two resources—people and time.

To maximise the potential of both, most managers need some reminders and basic guidelines to help them.

The Notes for Managers series provides succinct yet comprehensive coverage of key management issues and skills. The short time it takes to read each title will pay dividends in terms of utilising one of those key resources—people.

Whether we work in manufacturing industry, the service sector, a hospital, local government, or in the professions, our working conditions and the way in which we and our organisations act and behave must go through change at some point. Sometimes we are in control of these changes and sometimes they are imposed on us by anonymous 'market forces' or 'board policies'.

This book works from the premise that people will only be able to live with change, and organisations will only survive and remain competitive, if individuals are led through the change by their immediate boss—be it their director, manager, supervisor, chargehand or section head.

ALISTAIR GRAHAM
Director, The Industrial Society

1

CHANGE IS NORMAL

Change is normal, and is becoming more so. In our lives we move house more often than our parents. We move jobs; jobs that we thought were for life, cease to exist. Technology changes may radically alter our work. Economies boom and slump. Organisations expand and contract and structures change.

Much of this has always been so. However, the pace of change has accelerated. Few people, for instance, will not have been subject to some sort of structural change at work in the past few years. In many cases, this will have happened several times. The changes in technology in the last 20 years have been enormous and have occurred with increasing speed and in increasing number. The recession of the late 70s and early 80s imposed a need for rapid change in order to survive. Popular attitudes, including those towards work, have undergone a revolution since 1945.

The inevitability of change

It is, of course, futile to bemoan the facts. Our competitiveness depends upon our capacity to innovate and to keep pace with change. It may be possible to keep redundant jobs, industrial sites, or whole industries going by support and subsidy, but only by borrowing against future, imagined, prosperity. In any case, as individual managers and supervisors, we have little influence on the great issues. We are faced with a need, or an instruction, to effect change. Our job is to manage it: that we do this well is vital for two reasons. First, we are employed to run effective organisations, whether or not we personally like the changes that are

1

going on. Second, the satisfaction of those people we are responsible for depends upon our getting it right. For reasons both of efficiency and compassion we must manage change properly.

How, then, should we manage change? In the following chapters, nine areas for action are set out. The actions themselves are common sense and familiar to us all. What is important is to translate that common sense understanding into action. 'Sorry, I meant to consult you, but there wasn't enough time' will not remedy the disruption caused by such a failure to act.

The nine areas are as follows.

- *Explaining change*. Setting up systems for keeping everyone in the picture and explaining what is going on regularly and frequently.
- *Keeping control*. Making sure that we, as managers and supervisors, have up-to-date information and *really* know what is going on.
- *Ensuring commitment*. Selling change to the people for whom we are responsible. Gaining their enthusiasm and co-operation.
- *Coaching individual performance*. Jobs change in content and aims. Review these changes and help each person to develop the required skills and knowledge.
- *Taking decisions and delegating*. Getting decisions made close to the action. Consulting before we decide.
- *Training for change*. Training people to meet the new challenges.
- *What about the unions?* What needs to be negotiated and when? How should we go about consulting representatives?
- *Staying in touch*. Regularly walking around people's places of work. Looking after their physical and emotional well-being.
- *Learning from change*. Monitoring and evaluating; learning from success and failure.

2

EXPLAINING CHANGE

If people are to contribute well to the organisations that employ them, they need to know what is happening and why. High quality and productive work depends on people doing more than just obeying instructions. They must understand the importance of their work (however humble or routine it may seem) and be willing to give of their best.

This is true at all times. When rapid change takes place, the job of keeping people in the picture becomes both more difficult and more important. It becomes more difficult because many people fear change, as it may adversely affect their own working lives or those of their colleagues. It is more important because there is more to tell people.

There are many examples of major national organisations which have suffered considerable industrial problems by failing to sell the need for change to their own people. A more specific case is that of a manufacturing company in London which intended to sub-contract some tooling. This did not, in fact, threaten anyone's job. However, the tool-room only discovered the plans through the grapevine and immediately went on strike. What, then, needs to be done? People need to know what is going on:

- *regularly*—a systematic drill should be established so that everyone knows they will be briefed on, say, the first Monday of the month at 9.30 a.m.
- *face-to-face from their immediate boss*—enabling the message to be local and put in language that the team understands (face-to-face so questions can be asked and understanding checked)
- *relevantly*—on subjects which will help to raise the team's performance.

Team Briefing

Any supervisor or manager can set up a regular system of this sort. It can be helped greatly, however, by setting up a co-ordinated system of briefing, known as team briefing, for the whole of one site or one company (see the booklet of that title, in this series). This enables the managers at more senior levels to get consistent and simultaneous messages to all employees. Making this happen requires some extra action.

A short management brief needs to be written, indicating clearly those items which are compulsory and those that are optional. This written brief should be given to all briefers to avoid messages becoming distorted.

Timing must be as close to simultaneous at each level as can be managed. Otherwise, some people will have picked up one version from colleagues before hearing what their own boss has to say.

Despite this more co-ordinated approach, the primary aim is to put across local and relevant information. At each level, 70 per cent of the brief should still be specific to the team.

Finally, briefing should be brief—20 minutes with 10 minutes for questions should be adequate for most line managers and supervisors. If change itself tends to lengthen the brief, it is better to increase the frequency (from monthly to weekly, for instance) than to increase the length of each meeting by too much. People get bored very easily in meetings. The purpose of briefing is to keep them on our side, not to turn them off.

Although the above has put a lot of emphasis on face-to-face communication by immediate bosses, it also makes sense, during periods of change, to make sure other systems are working well. Is the noticeboard up-to-date, for instance? Was the new team structure in the company newsletter?

Most difficulties in managing change seem to have

something to do with failing to communicate properly. We must, therefore, treat this as a matter of the very highest priority.

Checklist

- Brief people regularly on progress, policy that affects them, changes in people and people's roles, and the action they must take.
- Keep a briefing file to build up on information they need.
- Support decisions once they have been made. It is our job to carry them out.
- Make someone responsible for a weekly check on the noticeboard.
- If there is a newsletter, use it to communicate messages about local changes to the rest of the organisation.

3

KEEPING CONTROL

In the previous chapter, we were concerned with the downward passage of information. If *telling* people what is going on is important it is also, of course, vital to *know* what is going on and be able to influence it. If we are to exercise this influence, our knowledge needs to be timely, relevant and accurate. If we are haphazard in the way in which we keep checks on the people and activities for which we are responsible, it is a problem at the best of times. When change is going on, this problem can all too easily escalate into things being wholly out of control. What is worse is that we may not know this until it is too late.

Knowing what is going on

Clearly, the information required by particular managers and supervisors will vary greatly depending on their role, level and industry. There do seem, however, to be some common hints which should help most of us.

Accountability

First, is accountability for people clear? Does every person in the organisation have a clear and singular answer to the question: 'Who is my boss?' If there is uncertainty about who is responsible for whom, it becomes much more difficult to keep any kind of check, as well as making it thoroughly confusing for the individual.

Particular areas to watch include the following.

● *Deputies*—is it really clear who reports to whom?

- *Over-large teams*—if an individual manager or super-visor is supposed to look after a team of more than 15, they will not be able to do it.
- *Secretaries and personal assistants*—are they as well informed as they should be, or do they sometimes get missed out because they have lower status than, for instance, the managers who report to a particular director?
- *Administrative or support staff*—where there is sometimes ambiguity about whether they report to a senior administrator or to the technical or professional people they do work for.
- *Positions*—where people may belong to a project team for the present but also belong to a specific department.

Clearly, most of us do not have the authority to completely redraw the structures we work in. If, however, there seems to be some confusion, we need to discuss it and sort out some more workable arrangement. Can, for instance, the supervisor with 25 people, ask the chargehand to look after 10 or 12 or them on a day-to-day basis?

Appraising

Second, do we see the individuals who work for us often enough to discuss their progress, consult them and set targets? Periods of change may well mean that some people require more help and direction to find the way through the changing demands of the job. A regular 20 minutes with each of them will help people towards solutions.

Progress reports

Third, what are the written records of progress like? Do we have one file that has an up-to-date summary of the essential facts and figures? This should either be in our hands or briefcase, or very readily accessible. Is it clear who is responsible for getting the weekly or monthly figures ready on time?

Checklist

- Sort out who is accountable to whom.
- Establish regular face-to-face checks with all individuals.
- Make sure you have an up-to-date summary of key figures and facts to hand.

4

ENSURING COMMITMENT

Whatever measures we, as managers and supervisors, may take to keep control over events, the people who finally affect the success or failure of change are those who actually have to carry it out. We have already discussed ways in which we can keep them better informed, and some ways we can be more up-to-date with the work they are doing and the problems they are meeting. What else could we be doing to ensure that, as change takes place, what needs to be done is done willingly and well?

It is important that people derive as much of a sense of achievement as possible from work, receive proper recognition for work done well, know the importance of the work they are doing, and feel that they are listened to. The problem is how to achieve this with real work, which may be mundane and boring and certainly contains unwelcome pressures, within the limited time that supervisors and managers have, particularly in times of change.

Delegation

Delegation is an immensely valuable tool which can both free the manager's time, and help to motivate staff. What is important, however, is that it is not used simply as a means of ridding ourselves of an endless series of trivial tasks. It is much better to delegate a sizeable chunk of authority to one individual, than several one-off tasks. Few people derive much satisfaction from the trivial, but many do from getting a large, and often difficult, job done well, even when that job involved some of those same one-off tasks.

Communication

Too many people seem to live in a 'no news is good news' world at work. Thanking people for work done well is the simplest, and probably the most under-used means of motivating them. Remember, too, that people will see constructive criticism as recognition. The mistake is to ignore people.

Target setting

Set targets, particularly where there are no ready-made milestones of achievement. For similar reasons clarify, and wherever possible show to people the end-product of their work, whether it is a physical object or a service. Targets should challenge people to higher performance. There is greater satisfaction in achieving against the odds.

Consultation

Always, except when immediate decisions are required, consult those affected by your decisions. This need not be too time consuming a process, especially if you have regular team and individual meetings available. Consulting people does not imply a search for consensus or compromise. It simply means you are prepared to listen sincerely to those views and then accept or reject them. The value of consultation is two-fold. First, it may produce ideas or information which you would not otherwise have taken into account. Second, most people like the chance to express what they think, even where the eventual decision does not always reflect their views.

Try to ensure that, as circumstances change, people's pay and physical conditions of work do not suffer and that everyone receives equitable treatment. It is even more important than usual that grievances receive prompt attention.

Checklist

- Delegate major areas of work.
- Recognise effort and criticise constructively.
- Set targets after consulting.
- Clarify the end product.
- Consult before you decide.

5

COACHING INDIVIDUAL PERFORMANCE

We have already mentioned that it may be helpful to see individuals on a regular basis. It is worth looking at these sessions in greater detail so that the greatest benefit can be obtained for both parties.

Annual performance reviews or appraisal systems may help in this process but, even in normal circumstances, more frequent review is often sensible. When jobs and job objectives are changing rapidly, frequent review becomes essential. Six main issues need to be clarified.

1   *Who is my boss?* Is it clear whose job it is to carry out the review? If structures have changed or people have been doing work for other managers, consult those other managers first but always keep to a one-to-one discussion.

2   *What is my job?* It is vital that the boss and job-holder have a compatible view of what results should be expected. Jobs are dynamic and no-one would wish people to wait for a formal discussion before doing what needs to be done. However, we do need to keep ourselves informed and make sure the right things are being done in the right way.

3   *What standard is expected?* It is helpful to provide people with yardsticks against which they can measure their own performance. Often these can be quantifiable, as in measures of volume or time-scale, but they may be more to do with an understanding of what good practice is. These yardsticks need to be brought up to date or priorities become very confused.

4 *How am I getting on?* Simply by clarifying standards you will be giving people a better picture of their own performance. It is, of course, also helpful to discuss them in order to praise good work and learn from it and to identify areas of difficulty and work together to improve on them.

5 *Where do I go in the future?* It is important to discuss direction of change for the department or section, and for the individual. What new skills need to be learnt? What old ones need developing? What potential new roles might make better use of someone's talents? It is, of course, a mistake to raise expectations which are not then fulfilled, but an honest discussion of expected changes before they take place can help to avoid sudden gaps appearing between available skills and required tasks. One of the unfortunate consequences of failing to coach and develop existing staff can be expensive 'buying-in' of outside skills.

6 *How do I get there?* Having discussed the current and future positions, targets need to be set. 'Set' is the right word, rather than 'agreed', because it is the boss's job to make the final decision. The best targets, nonetheless, often come from suggestions made by job-holders. The drill is to consult the job-holder then set the target. Avoid setting too many (five or six will help to clarify priorities, 23 will not) and avoid them all being aimed at the same date.

The whole process is designed to help people to come to terms with change at work, to develop the skills and knowledge that are needed, and to understand how they fit into new patterns of work. It is our job to coach and advise our people through change.

Checklist

- Set out who is responsible for each person's performance.
- Set up regular discussions of performance.
- Identify the key results expected from each job.
- Set a clearly understood standard.
- Identify areas for improvement (including those that are already good).
- Discuss change and its impact on each job.
- Set and monitor targets.

6

TAKING DECISIONS AND DELEGATING

Team leaders always have to take decisions. Good ones always delegate. The difference that change makes is that it implants greater urgency. In particular, the need for decisions may become almost overwhelming. Even though some of the decisions seem small in themselves, they intrude upon other more important work because they have deadlines attached. We find it difficult to delegate this work because, again, there is little time and it can take more time to explain something to somebody else than to do it oneself.

A manager managing change like this is doing nobody any good. The task will be accomplished badly, time-scales will slip and members of the team will resent the boss keeping so much to him or herself. Lastly, but by no means least importantly, managers will harm both their health and career. What is needed is a more prepared and systematic approach.

Delegate

If in doubt, delegate but, wherever and whenever possible, do it early. If subordinates have the preparation required to handle an area of decision-making before change accelerates, then they can handle the problem. Constructive use of performance coaching, discussed in the last chapter, will help. Remember that decisions made closer to the action are usually better ones, provided the limits are clearly defined. Try to avoid delegating then continually interfering. This will only waste your time and earn the fully justified resentment of your team. Set up a sensible monitoring system, have an occasional impromptu look, and take the risk.

Having to decide

If you are unable to delegate (and, of course, some responsibilities, for example, discipline, can never be delegated) how should you approach a decision?

First, consider the problem. By when must a decision be made? Get hold of all the facts you can. Clearly, the amount of information you can bear in mind is partly a function of the time-scale. If a decision must be made, it must be made with the best possible facts.

Second, consult. If people are affected by your decision, you must try and consult them. If it is impossible to get to them during the day, try ringing them in the evening. Most people will prefer an interrupted evening to a decision made, apparently, 'over their head'. Also try to get to those who may not be affected, but may have useful ideas. Try to bounce your own ideas off somebody, at least.

Third, make up your mind. Look at all the information you have put together, sleep on it if time allows, and decide. If the issue appears marginal, take the course of action requiring greater courage. You have probably slightly biased your thinking against 'difficult' decisions.

Fourth, tell everybody. Do this face-to-face to all the people, together if possible. If these people need to pass the message further down the line, back it up in writing.

Last, check that your decision has been carried out. Staff will soon realise if you are the sort of boss who issues instructions but fails to follow them up.

If all this seems too time-consuming, it may mean you need to look at delegating more. It may also mean you sometimes have to short-circuit the process in an emergency. Whatever else, always make sure people are informed as quickly as possible.

Checklist

- Delegate areas of authority before large-scale change.
- Identify a time-scale and assemble information.
- Consult those affected.
- Decide. If in doubt, take the courageous course.
- Inform everybody.
- Check your decision has been carried out.

7

TRAINING FOR CHANGE

It is all too easy to see training as a specialist function divorced from the normal duties and responsibilities of managers and supervisors. There are, however, three compelling reasons for regarding training as a critical area. First, most of what we learn, we learn by doing. Structured experience is the most effective means of raising levels of skill and knowledge. Second, the level of ability of our team is of direct consequence to us and it is, therefore, up to us to influence it. Third, change demands a quick training response. The speed of response requires local initiative.

How to do it

Yet again, information is important. It is often helpful to have some sort of central record of who can do what, as well as a record in individual files. A simple chart will enable the manager to see, at a glance, where the gaps are. Records should include formal internal and external training courses and skills obtained 'on-the-job'.

Do not assume that you should carry out all the local training yourself. You are unlikely to have the time to do it properly, and there may be more expert people in your team. Remember to look around the rest of the organisation for the expertise you are after.

Of course, use formal training courses if they seem appropriate and finances allow. Much of the possible benefits will be lost, however, if the training is not applied properly to the work itself. In order to combat this danger, take the following course of action.

1   Find out exactly what the course teaches and how. Ring up the course providers if this is unclear. Is it for the right level of staff? Does it broadly meet your need?
2   Brief the trainee on what you expect.
3   Debrief the trainee on his or her return. Discuss the actions required to put the training into effect. Fit these in with existing targets. Can you use the trained person to train others at work?

Resistance to training

You may, of course, find some resistance to training. This may simply be fear of the unknown, or it may be a genuine difficulty in adapting to the demands of a changed job. In the former case, good, frequent, coaching sessions will help. People who find the eventual radical change difficult to accept, may see each short-term step as less daunting. This is often particularly so with experienced people who are expected to change long established methods and patterns of work. There will be more, sad, instances of total inability to adapt, which will need to be dealt with compassionately. If, however, change is a matter of necessity, it may be that some redundancy is unavoidable. Every effort should have been spent in training and counselling to help people adapt or find new roles within the organisation.

Training is a matter of survival. If organisations are to adapt, the people must be helped to adapt, and this needs to be explained to them.

Checklist

● Keep a record of who can do what.
● Use your own team and others in your organisation as trainers.
● Brief and debrief for training courses.
● Set step-by-step targets to help people change skills.
● Highlight training in regular briefing.

8

WHAT ABOUT THE UNIONS?

Trade unions are often associated with resistance to change. Public attention has been drawn to disputes in the printing and mining industries. Alongside these well-publicised conflicts, vast areas of industry, commerce, and the public services have gone through major structural or technological change without significant industrial relations problems.

It is futile to bemoan the influence of trade unions. A high proportion of the working population is unionised and, despite falls in membership in recent years, this looks certain to remain so. Indeed, in some areas with little tradition of union membership (the finance industry, for example) there has been growth in membership. Those of us who manage in organisations where unions are recognised, need to discover what to do to reduce disruption, increase co-operation, and maintain constructive relations with unions through periods of change.

Communication and industrial relations

When looking at past instances where gaining union co-operation while managing change has proved difficult, one issue crops up again and again. A large local authority, for example, wanted to introduce job evaluation at the same time as reductions in overall staffing. Despite the existence of regular consultative meetings, this innovation was not mentioned until after its introduction had begun. As a result, people refused to co-operate on other issues and the scheme's introduction was delayed by several months. Communication, then, is often the heart of the problem.

Two lines of communication need working on. First, we need to establish good, regular, communication through the management line, as described in Chapter 2. We cannot expect the unions to deliver the management message for us. Second, we need a systematic approach to consulting staff and their representatives and, where appropriate, negotiating with them.

Of crucial importance is the relationship between first-line supervisors and union representatives. If these two see each other regularly and are used to sorting out problems themselves, it will be possible to deal with grievances, which are an almost inevitable product of change, before they develop into major issues. To this end it may be useful to provide some training for both supervisors and representatives.

Where consultative committees exist, managers should use them, not just to assess reaction to proposed changes, but also to gather ideas about how to proceed in everyone's best interest. Make sure issues brought to such committees by management are already being briefed to managers and supervisors. Otherwise managers will discover their boss's proposals from their subordinates.

If there are changes to terms and conditions which need to be negotiated, start as early as possible. Having to negotiate against a tight deadline may lead to your giving away on issues where you should stand firm. Be very clear about what is negotiable and what is not.

All these actions assume the existence of clear written procedural agreements. Have a look at these and see if they are robust and sensible enough to work when change is going on apace.

Checklist

- Organise regular representative/supervisor contact.
- Train representatives and supervisors.
- Consult early and genuinely seek ideas.
- Negotiate before the pressure is on. Stick to your guns.
- Look at written procedures. Renegotiate them if they are unclear or impose too much delay.

9

STAYING IN TOUCH

It is very easy for the modern manager to become office and paper-bound (or, perhaps, terminal-bound). The larger the organisation and the more senior the manager, the greater is the risk of losing touch with the shop-floor or its equivalent. In periods of rapid change, this can get worse. There may appear to be simply too much to do to keep in contact with the people for whom we are responsible. However, if we rely only on systematic information, we will not get the whole truth. We need both to see and be seen.

Walk the job

At any time, it is the job of the leader to regularly walk round each person's place of work in order to observe, listen and praise. This should include areas which report to supervisors, and managers who report to you and to your middle managers. This is not intended to undermine the intermediate leaders, but merely to know better what is going on. Indeed, it is bad practice to interfere unless an immediate danger is posed. (A physically dangerous practice obviously demands immediate intervention, for example.) The senior manager should note things of concern and then talk to the supervisor or manager of the area.

When things are changing quickly, increase the frequency of these walkabouts. If the offices were moved around at the weekend go and see what it looks like on Monday morning. How do people feel about the new arrangements? Walk the job on the night shift. Check how well people are kept informed by their own immediate bosses. How positively have the changes been explained to them?

Be involved

Work alongside people. As the immediate team leader this should be a regular and frequent part of your job. If new tasks have to be undertaken, find out for yourself how difficult, boring or time-consuming they are. Show you care about the physical conditions people work in. As a more senior manager, still do this from time to time. Apart from the impressions you make, you will be told things when working with someone that you would never find out any other way.

Do it properly

Do not rely on good intentions to do any of this. If we simply try to 'fit it in' to an already tight schedule, it will not happen. Set a frequency standard and block off time in your diary. When changes happen, make sure part of the plan includes our physical presence both during and immediately after the biggest alterations.

Attend social functions with your staff. This may or may not be the natural inclination of a particular manager or supervisor, but it is undoubtedly their job. Even when change is forced by economic hardship, try to organise some sort of social event. (If money is genuinely tight, make sure it is self-financing. People will resent subsidies for parties when others are losing their jobs, for example.)

Change is often seen, at the bottom of organisations, as something done by 'them' to 'us'. However unfair this view, counteract it by sharing the experience at the bottom.

Checklist

- Regularly walk round each person's place of work. Listen to their views and praise good work.

- Identify problems to team leaders concerned, not the individuals.
- Work alongside people.
- Set out a frequency. Increase it when change occurs.
- Attend and organise social functions.

10

LEARNING FROM CHANGE

Change must involve both risk and experiment. However good our planning may be, we cannot guarantee success. We have to prepare ourselves, therefore, not only to keep a check on what is happening, but also to alter our plans. If we have splendid monitoring systems, but carry on monitoring failure, we will not have done our jobs. We may also lose all credibility in the eyes of our staff if we remain wedded to an unworkable development simply because we thought of it.

Reviewing the change

In particular, it is helpful to set out a review period. If, for instance, we are changing structures in some parts of the organisation, set up a meeting of the accountable managers for, say, the three months after the changes. Are we achieving what we intended to achieve? Are results better? If the changes are working, how can they be improved? Should similar changes be used elsewhere in the organisations? There are, of course, occasions when the whole thing should be abandoned and we should revert to the old system before more time and money are wasted.

Avoid inventing the wheel twice. If a change works in one part of an organisation, after inevitable teething troubles, get the good practice clear and written down so others will encounter fewer problems.

Altering the plan

Make sure changes of plan are explained quickly to all those who are affected. It may be difficult, having enthused about a development three months before, to be equally convincing about a radical change to it. It is, nonetheless, our responsibility to do so if we are to have any chance of the changes being carried out well. Always explain why plans have been changed. People may well resent such shifts of policy but will find them easier to accept if they know the reasons. If we do not know the reasons ourselves we should pester our bosses until we have some convincing arguments.

Checklist

- Review the success of changes. Set up review meetings.
- Be prepared to alter plans.
- Write down good practice.
- Explain why plans have changed.

11

ACTION FOR THE FUTURE

What must we do, then, to manage change well?

- Accept that change is normal and increasing. Help others to accept this.
- Keep good, simple, information systems.
- Delegate, set targets, praise good work.
- See everyone regularly as individuals. Coach and re-target as jobs change.
- If you are unable to delegate, consult before you decide.
- Train in anticipation of change.
- Keep union representatives informed. Consult and negotiate early.
- Walk around and listen to people. Work alongside them.
- Evaluate change. Alter plans if need be.